Cryptocurrency Trading Tips and Strategies for Beginners

How to Make Money with Cryptocurrency and Succeed with It

Introduction

Congratulations on purchasing this book and thank you for doing so.

These days, so many people are eager to learn how to make money by investing or trading cryptocurrencies. Every day, you can read news about different cryptocurrencies and how their prices increase by a significant percentage. In fact, many professional investors in stocks and bonds have switched to investing in cryptocurrencies. Indeed, the cryptocurrency market is revolutionizing how investments are made. If you want to learn how to invest in a market where you can make 100% or even 2,000% profit (or even higher) in a short period of time, then this is the book for you.

The following chapters will teach you the ins and outs of investing in and trading cryptocurrencies for profit:

Chapter 1 discusses the basics so that you will have a good foundation and understanding of what cryptocurrencies are all about.

Chapter 2 teaches the different kinds of cryptocurrency wallets. Before you can start using cryptocurrencies, you first need to have a place where you can store them.

Chapter 3 lays down the set standard and criteria to look for in a cryptocurrency trading broker.

Chapter 4 reveals the powerful strategies that you can use to turn the odds in your favor and increase your chances of making a profit.

Chapter 5 talks about cryptocurrency mining, which is another way of investing in and earning cryptocurrencies.

Chapter 6 discusses the best investing and trading practices used by highly successful and professional investors/traders. Turn these practices into a habit to significantly increase your winning edge.

May this book be your guiding light to success and financial freedom.

There are plenty of books on this subject on the market, thanks again for choosing this one! Every effort was made to ensure it is full of as much useful information as possible. Please enjoy!

TABLE OF CONTENTS

Chapter 1

Cryptocurrency Basics

What is a *Cryptocurrency*?

Cryptocurrency is a form of digital cash that has high security. It is stored electronically (online); therefore, it does not have a physical existence. In most cases, a high level of anonymity is also enjoyed by its users. It functions as a substitute for money but also offers other interesting features. It is secured using cryptography, which refers to the process of converting information into codes. Cryptography was used during the Second World War when it was important for an army to ensure the privacy and security of communication against enemies. As the world evolved into the digital and computer era, cryptography found its application in the world of cryptocurrency.

To date, there are more than 900 cryptocurrencies that have already been created. It should be noted that the first and still the number one cryptocurrency in the world is Bitcoin. As of December 28, 2017, the price of 1 bitcoin is more than USD 15,000.

Why Should You Invest in Cryptocurrency?

Although a cryptocurrency normally functions as a substitute for money, it is noteworthy that people who possess cryptocurrencies do not always use them as such. These days, many people own cryptocurrencies as a form of investment. This is because putting your money in cryptocurrencies can be a very lucrative investment. Unlike investing in stocks where an annual profit of 30% is already considered high, you can profit by more than 200% (or even more) in a month's time when you invest in cryptocurrency. In fact, there are already many people around the world who have earned millions just by investing in cryptocurrencies. Even if you compare it with other investments, it is easy to realize that investing in cryptocurrency is most likely the best option that can help you achieve financial freedom. This is also the reason why many investors in stocks, bonds, and real estate, have turned to investing in cryptocurrencies.

So, just how much profit can you make? One of the benefits of investing in this kind of asset is that you can earn as little as you want and also as high as you want. The cryptocurrency market has a very high volatility. Unfortunately, this is why some investors are still cautious of investing in cryptocurrencies. However, if you come to think of it, it is exactly this highly volatile nature of cryptocurrencies that makes it a very lucrative investment. It is what allows its price to increase by more than 500% in a short span of time.

Investing in cryptocurrencies is also open to everyone. Since it is held electronically, all you need is an Internet access, and you can manage your account and make transactions with just a few clicks of a mouse. Everything happens online, and you are in full control of your investment. You also do not have to invest a big amount of money. In fact, there are real-life success stories where a few hundred dollar investment turned into a multi-million dollar profit. Here is a classic example: Had you invested even just $300 in the cryptocurrency, bitcoin, way back in 2009 or early 2010, then you would have been a multimillionaire by now.

Of course, just like any other kind of investment, there are risks involved when you invest in any cryptocurrency. It is not a secret that the price of a cryptocurrency can drop significantly if the market does not support it. Legal and economic factors can also affect the price of a cryptocurrency. There is also a growing competition among the different cryptocurrencies. Therefore, to avoid losing your investment and increase the chances of making a nice profit, you should do your research and analyze the cryptocurrency market properly. The fact remains that even today, investing in cryptocurrency proves to be highly lucrative. This is why so many people these days are so eager to learn how to break into the cryptocurrency market and rake in serious amounts of profit.

Investing in Cryptocurrency vs. Gambling

Is investing in cryptocurrency similar to gambling in a casino? The answer will depend on how you approach the cryptocurrency market. If you just make investments and rely heavily on luck, then you are gambling. This is also not a suggested approach. But, if you do your research and make an analysis of the market, if you are willing to exert time and effort to come up with a sound investment decision, then you are no longer gambling but investing. Unlike gambling where the outcome is randomly made, the changes in the price of cryptocurrencies are not random. In fact, if you have the right information, then you will be more likely to predict the movement of a particular cryptocurrency. You can then take appropriate actions to take advantage of it and make a profit.

Blockchain Technology

Blockchain technology, or simply blockchain, is the backbone technology of Bitcoin, as well as other cryptocurrencies. It is composed of a chain of records known as blocks. Once a block is added to the chain, there is no way of canceling, altering, or withdrawing it, except with the consent of a majority of the users in the blockchain network. The network is spread over a vast network of computers. All cryptocurrency transactions are public and viewable over the blockchain. The blockchain is a public and distributed ledger that records all transactions. It is also decentralized, which means that no central authority or organization can influence or manipulate it. Hence, it can be trusted by all its users.

The blockchain technology also offers a high security. For an attack against the blockchain to be successful, the attack must have at least 51% of the total hash rate of the entire blockchain. Since the blockchain is spread over a wide network kg computers, it would be impossible for an attack to have 51% of the power rate of the network. Take note that this does not mean that the blockchain can no longer be attacked. Rather, it means that the attack will not be successful. Also, even if the attack possesses the said 51% hash rate of the blockchain network concerned, there is still no assurance that it will be successful.

As far as the blockchain technology is concerned, there is also what is referred to as a *private* blockchain where the network can be controlled and influenced by a designated group, individual, or organization. However, it is noteworthy that bitcoin and other known cryptocurrency networks use a public and decentralized blockchain network.

Bitcoin and Other Cryptocurrencies (Altcoins)

Bitcoin is the number one and most successful cryptocurrency in the market. It has become the leading standard that other cryptocurrencies have been categorized as mere altcoins, which is short for alternative coins. However, this does not mean that investing in altcoins is no longer lucrative. In fact, there are many altcoins out there that increase in price by more than 500% in just a short period of time.

There is a growing competition among the different cryptocurrencies in the market. Gone are the days when you can just offer any cryptocurrency and expect for it to be successful. Today, a cryptocurrency has to be seen as something valuable by the market to draw attention and interest. This is why altcoins usually come up with interesting features other than being used as a substitute for money. For example, the cryptocurrency known as Ethereum which is currently the second most successful cryptocurrency next to bitcoin promotes the use of smart contracts and application on its blockchain. Another example is the cryptocurrency known as Ripple which helps banks to make faster transactions and processes at a lower cost. Other cryptocurrencies like Dash and Zcash offer higher privacy and make transactions completely private.

When investing, it is best to look for a cryptocurrency that offers value. But, of course, value alone is not enough. The cryptocurrency must also be promoted effectively; otherwise, the market will not even know that it exists. Last but not least, you should pay attention to the market acceptance of a cryptocurrency. You can measure this by paying attention to how the market responds when a certain cryptocurrency is being promoted. Therefore, you should always be updated with the latest news and developments in the cryptocurrency market.

Legal Concerns

Cryptocurrencies usually have a decentralized network. This means that no central organization or authority regulates them. Generally, cryptocurrencies are legal; however, this does not mean that governments can no longer regulate the use of cryptocurrencies within their jurisdiction. After all, governments must serve and protect its people. There are still a few countries like Ecuador and Bolivia where the use of cryptocurrencies is considered illegal. This is not hard to understand considering that cryptocurrency users enjoy a high level of privacy considering that the transactions are anonymous in nature. Hence, cryptocurrencies can be used in the commission of crimes, especially in money laundering.

Not all states share the same stand with respect to the use of cryptocurrencies. The good news is that in most states, cryptocurrencies are completely legal. Some time ago, Russia outlawed the use of cryptocurrencies in its territory; however, Russia has already changed its position and now accepts the use of cryptocurrencies. Singapore even declared that it does not impose any regulation on the use of cryptocurrencies. In the Philippines, bitcoin can be used to pay for electric, water, and other bills. As time goes on, more and more people are being open to the use of cryptocurrencies. Of course, this does not mean that governments can no longer regulate the use of cryptocurrencies. If a government finds it necessary, it may impose regulations as to the use of cryptocurrencies within its jurisdiction. At present, it can be said that governments are still on the lookout as to the possible effects of cryptocurrencies. As a cryptocurrency trader/investor, it is important for you to follow on the news, especially as to the latest government regulations on the subject. For example, when Russia legalize the use of bitcoin, the price of bitcoin increased. But, when China declared that it would close down all its local cryptocurrency exchanges, the price of bitcoin experienced a significant decrease in price. As you can see, how a state reacts to bitcoin and other cryptocurrencies can play a significant effect upon the prices of the different cryptocurrencies in the market.

Chapter 2

The Different Kinds
of Cryptocurrency Wallets

Hot Wallet vs. Cold Wallet

Before you can even start investing in or trading cryptocurrencies, the first step is for you to have a cryptocurrency wallet. A cryptocurrency wallet is where you store your cryptocurrencies. Now, there are different kinds of cryptocurrency wallets. You should know their differences so that you will know which wallet type is most suitable for your needs. Generally, there are only two kinds of cryptocurrency wallets. There is a hot wallet and a cold wallet. On the one hand, a hot wallet is the kind of cryptocurrency wallet that exists online. Hence, it is very convenient to use. On the other hand, a cold wallet is the kind of cryptocurrency wallet that is stored offline. Although it is not as convenient to use as a hot wallet, a cold wallet offers greater security since it is not exposed to the Internet. Now, let us take a look at the specific types of cryptocurrency wallets.

➢ Web Wallet

A web wallet is the most common type of cryptocurrency hot wallet. It is the most widely used wallet. It is also referred to as an online wallet. As the name already implies, a web wallet is the kind of cryptocurrency wallet that is accessible on the World Wide Web. A good example of a web wallet is Coinbase.

➢ Mobile Wallet

A mobile wallet is another type of hot wallet. It is the type of hot wallet that you can download on your mobile device. Many web wallets also have a mobile version. Therefore, it is not unusual to find a web wallet that is also a mobile wallet at the same time. Again, a good example of this would be Coinbase. It is a hot wallet that has an online presence, as well as a mobile feature.

➢ Desktop Wallet

A desktop wallet is a kind of cold wallet. Hence, it is stored offline. When you use a desktop wallet, you store your cryptocurrency in a computer. Although called as a desktop wallet, the computer that you use does not necessarily have to be a desktop computer. It can also be a laptop, as long as it has a functioning Operating System.

When you use a desktop wallet, you should remember that the computer that you use should not be connected to the Internet. The reason is that once something is connected to the Internet, there is an exposure to risks and possibility of getting hacked. Also, before you use a computer as a desktop wallet, it is strongly suggested that you reformat it to remove bugs and viruses.

➢ Hardware Wallet

A hardware wallet is also like a desktop wallet. It is also a cold wallet, but instead of storing your cryptocurrencies in a computer, you get to store them in some hardware device, such as a USB. Just like a desktop computer, you should avoid connecting your hardware wallet to a computer that is connected to the Internet.

➢ Paper Wallet

A paper wallet is a kind of cold wallet where you store your private and public keys on a paper. It is a good practice to print several copies of your keys and be sure to keep them in a safe place. Most paper wallets will give you a QR code that you can scan before you can access your wallet online. This way you can rest for sure that your cryptocurrencies are protected since a person will have to get a copy of the codes that you have printed on a paper before he can access your cryptocurrencies which are stored online.

Which Wallet Type Should You Use?

The right Waller type for you will depend on how you want to use cryptocurrencies. If you intend to make a series of transactions on a regular basis, then a got wallet would be more suitable for you. But, if you just want to invest in a particular cryptocurrency for a long-term, then a cold wallet would be more suitable. If you want, you can use both kinds of cryptocurrency wallets. It is not uncommon to find cryptocurrency investors and traders who use both hot and cold wallets.

It is worth noting that hot wallets have already improved their security. In fact, many professional cryptocurrency investors these days only use a hot wallet. Still, when it comes to the security of your cryptocurrencies, a cold wallet offers the highest level of security.

Cryptocurrency Wallet Security Protection Tips

There are some things that you should observe to keep your cryptocurrency wallet safe and secure. The first important thing that you should do is to use a strong password. Your wallet's password is your first defense against anyone would access your account without permission. Make sure that you use a strong password. A common mistake is to mcct only the minimum requirement. Hence, do not just use six characters. Use at least 10 characters as your password. You should also combine upper and lower case letters. Also, use numbers and symbols. Needless to say, do not use your name or date of birth as your password. Instead, use something that other people will not be able to guess correctly. It is also a good practice to change your password from time to time.

You should also check if the page is secure before you enter any sensitive information, such as your password. It is easy to know if a page is secure or not. Just look at the URL bar, and you should see a green padlock and the word "Secure" written on the left side of the URL bar. Never input any sensitive information unless the page is secure.

A cryptocurrency wallet is usually able to generate a new wallet address. Take note that a single cryptocurrency wallet can generate multiple wallet addresses for free. Cryptocurrency transactions are anonymous in nature in the sense that your name and other personal information will not be revealed on the chain. Instead, what you will see would be the wallet address that issues by the sender and the receiving wallet address of the receiver. You can also see the amount. However, the names and other personal details of the parties involved remain confidential. You should make it a habit of requesting a new wallet address for every new transaction that you make. A wallet address is like a string of random letters and numbers. By always requesting a new wallet address, you can minimize your exposure online. Do not worry; creating a new wallet address is free of charge, and all it takes is a just a few clicks of a mouse.

Remember not to access your cryptocurrency wallet when you are connected to a public Wi-Fi. Public Wi-Fi's are unsecured. Some hackers take advantage of public Wi-Fi's, so be sure to exercise caution. When connected to a public Wi-Fi, never access your cryptocurrency wallet even if you see that the page has a green padlock.

If you happen to have lots of cryptocurrencies, but you only want to use a hot wallet, a suggested way is to keep them in separate hot wallets. This way you can spread and effectively minimize your risks. Do not keep all your cryptocurrencies in a single wallet if you have a big amount of cryptocurrencies.

If you are using a cold wallet, you should understand that although a cold wallet is more secure than a hot wallet, it does not mean that a cold wallet is completely invulnerable to attacks. Keep in mind that a cold wallet can still be stolen and broken. Although a cold wallet may not have to worry about online threats, physical threats should be a concern. Therefore, you should make sure to keep your cold wallet in a safe place. Also, you should use a well-functioning cold wallet. It would be a problem if your cold wallet suddenly gets broken or if it malfunctions. Always consider the quality of your cold wallet.

Chapter 3

Cryptocurrency Broker

If you want to trade cryptocurrencies, you have to open an account with a reliable cryptocurrency trading broker. Now, by simply searching online, you will find lots of brokers that seem to offer the same services. So, how do you know which broker you should use and will best suit your needs? Here is a set of standards to look for:

Latest ratings and reviews

Before you despair any real money or cryptocurrency in your trading account, you should first check the latest ratings and reviews of your chosen broker as given by other traders. Doing this is easy. Simply use your favorite browser, type the name of the broker, and add the word "reviews." Press the enter key and wait for the search engine results page (SERP) to give you a list of related pages. Read as many reviews as you cab from different websites and reviewers. Also, pay attention to the dates of the most recent reviews. It is also not uncommon for a broker to hire freelance writers to come up with a positive review regarding their service, so do not rely on a single website for reviews. Do not rush this part as it is important for you to work with a broker that is reliable and trustworthy. Remember to work only with a legitimate and reliable tradingbroker. Not to mention, there are scammers out there who only want to steal your money/cryptocurrencies.

Deposit and withdrawal limits and requirements

Find out the minimum and maximum limit for making a deposit and withdrawal. Also, it is common for brokers to ask for a copy of certain documents before they process a withdrawal. Be sure that you have these documents available in your possession; otherwise, you run the risk of having your cryptocurrencies locked in your trading account without any way of withdrawing them or turning them into real money. Make sure that you know the requirements of your broker. It is fairly easy to make a deposit, but it can be hard to make a withdrawal. Be very clear about this part with your broker. If you have questions, do not hesitate to contact the customer support team. You should also check how many days it would take for your broker to completely process a withdrawal. Ideally, it should not take more than 24 hours for a broker to complete a withdrawal request, especially if you have already submitted the required documents if any. Normally, a broker will just request a copy of some identity documents, such as a valid ID and a proof of billing with your name and address printed on it.

Fees

Check the fees that your broker may impose. Is there a trading fee? Is there a fixed amount that is imposed or is there a certain percentage? Also, check how much is the withdrawal fee. Pay attention to other fees that your broker might impose.

Customer support

It is important for you to work with a broker that has an active and professional customer support team. Find out the ways that your broker offers on how to keep in touch with the support team. Normally, there is an email address that you can contact, or you can even send a message directly to the broker's trading platform. Your brawler may also provide you with a number that you can call or even an on-page love char support. Also, check the schedule as to the availability of the customer support.

Simply knowing how to contact the customer support team is not enough. You should as also find out if it is responsive and helpful enough. The best way to do this is by testing it. Before you even deposit any cryptocurrency into your trading account, contact the customer support team and ask any question. A good question will be if there are any substitute documents that you may submit in case the documents that they require to approve a withdrawal request are not available. Of course, you can ask any question or inquiry that you may have. Pay attention to how fast, and professional the support team resolves your inquiry. Ideally, you should get a solution or at least a clarificatory reply within 24 hours. As a cryptocurrency investor or trader, it is important that you work with a broker that has a highly professional customer support team.

Cryptocurrencies being traded

Check the cryptocurrencies that are available for trading. Of course, the more cryptocurrencies that your broker provides, the more choices that you will have. Ideally, your broker should also make available the not so known altcoins. After all, many of these unpopular altcoins also increase in price significantly. Hence, if you are a trader, you should also keep your eyes on them. Some of these altcoins have even increased by more than 1,000%.

Trading platform

Your broker should provide you with a professionally designed trading platform. Although design itself is not that important, it also helps to set the mood for trading. The trading platform should also provide you with tools that you need, such as graphs and charts, to help you come up with a sound trading decision. The platform should also be easy and convenient to use. All in all it should make the trading experience easier and more comfortable for you.

Bonuses

Check if the broker offers useful bonuses and/or promos. Bonuses or promos are not really required, but they can be helpful. Just be careful before you accept any bonus or promo since it usually comes with a catch. For example, there is usually a requirement that you need to meet before you can make a withdrawal. Unfortunately, such requirement is not always easy to satisfy. Therefore, before you accept and bonus or promo, be sure that the terms and conditions of the bonus are clear to you. In case of doubt, feel free to contact the customer support team.

Margin trading

A trading broker may also allow you to do margin trading. Margin trading is where you can borrow cryptocurrencies from the broker so that you can trade and hopefully profit a higher amount. Of course, since you will be borrowing cryptocurrencies from your broker, you will have to pay your broker a certain interest. Normally, a broker may allow you to margin trade more than 50% of your invested capital. Find out how much you can margin trade and the interest imposed by your broker. Take note that if you are a beginner, it is advised that you should avoid margin trading.

Mobile version

These days, it is easier and quicker to access the Internet using your mobile phone. Hence, your broker should allow you to access the trading platform directly from your mobile device. You should be able to manage your account and open and close positions using your mobile phone. Your broker should also make it easy and convenient for you to do this. The important parts of the trading platform should be easily accessible on your mobile device. The mobile version should be as convenient, if not more convenient, as the desktop version.

A note about using a trading broker

You are not always required to use a trading broker. If you intend to trade cryptocurrencies, then you need a trading broker. However, if you just want to invest, say, in bitcoin, especially if it is a long-term investment, then all you need is to get a cryptocurrency wallet. There are cryptocurrency wallets like Coinbase and coins.ph that allow their users to buy bitcoins directly from the wallet itself. Hence, if you just want to make a long-term investment in bitcoin, then you might just get a bitcoin wallet and skip the party where you need to use a trading broker.

Also, before you purchase any cryptocurrency, whether from a broker, directly through your cryptocurrency wallet, or otherwise, you should check the current market price of the cryptocurrency that you want to buy.The reason is that there are individuals and companies out there that sell cryptocurrencies at a premium price. You should check the current market price to be sure that you are getting a fair deal for your money, especially if it is tour first time to buy cryptocurrencies. Take note that there is a difference between the buy price and sell price. The buy price is always higher than the sell price. Obviously, when buying a cryptocurrency, you should focus on the buy price.

Chapter 4

Powerful Strategies

Fundamental Analysis

When it comes to any form of investing, fundamental analysis us something that you should definitely learn. Many people consider it as the lifeblood of investment. Where he investing in cryptocurrency, stocks, or bonds, this type of analysis always plays a vital role to your success. So, what is fundamental analysis? As the name implies, it deals with the "fundamentals" or the basics. They are important because the basics significantly influence the priced of cryptocurrencies. But, what exactly are the basic elements? How do you identify them from the bulk of information that you can read online? When you use fundamental analysis, you should focus on the latest news on cryptocurrencies. You should also pay attention to news about the economy, technology, government regulations, and others, that may influence the cryptocurrency market. Basically, fundamental analysis is about gathering and analyzing information. Take note that the more information that you have, especially if you have high-quality information, the easier it will be for you to predict the price movements of the cryptocurrencies in the market.

Fundamental analysis can also be combined with other strategies. In fact, if you consider yourself a professional cryptocurrency investor or trader, it is a *must* that you always apply fundamental analysis regardless of your preferred strategy for investing. After all, fundamental analysis would not harm you but can significantly help you come up with a sound investment/trading decision. Applying fundamental analysis is also what makes your investment different from gambling. Indeed, with the proper use of this strategy, you can effectively turn the odds in your favor.

Thanks to the Internet, you can easily get valuable information online. Just do not be lazy to do your research and analyze the news and other data that you can get. Also, pay attention to the numbers. For example, if you get a lead that shows that a particular cryptocurrency has increased by 50% in value, do not just be content with knowing that it increased by 50%. Expand your research and look at its specific value, as well as its price behavior. Fundamental analysis is not just about knowing what has already been revealed to the public; you should also dig in and make your own analysis.

Technical Analysis

Technical analysis is used by many cryptocurrency investors and traders. If you are more of a visual person and enjoy analyzing graphs and charts, then technical analysis is the one for you. With technical analysis, you will be dealing with the price movements as reflected by the graphs and charts. The idea behind this approach is that all the different factors that affect a cryptocurrency have their final influence on the price. Therefore, by simply dealing with the price movement alone, you get to analyze the many factors that affect a cryptocurrency all at once. Also, regardless of how many factors that you analyze, it is still the price movement of a cryptocurrency that will determine whether or not you will make a profit.

The key to using technical analysis is to be able to identify patterns. Indeed, patterns do exist. However, you should remember that patterns come and go. Therefore, do not expect to see a pattern every time that you look at a chart or graph. But, if ever you see one, then you should take advantage of it.

Many investors and traders love using technical analysis. Just like fundamental analysis, this strategy can also be used in combination with another strategy or strategies. In fact, it is suggested that you apply technical analysis with fundamental analysis.

There are many sites online that will provide you with live graphs to show the price movements of the different cryptocurrencies in the market. Do not worry; every trustworthy broker will provide you with some trading tools such as the graphs that you need for technical analysis on its trading platform for free.

Averaging Down

This strategy is a good way to earn a big amount of profit. Take note, however, that this is considered an aggressive approach, so use it carefully and wisely. Averaging down will allow you to purchase a cryptocurrency at a "bargain" which you can then sell for profit after some time. It is not really a "bargain" in the literal sense of the word. Here is an example to illustrate how this strategy works: Let us say that you want to invest in bitcoin. Let us assume that the price of bitcoin is USD 10,000. You make a buy order at the said price of USD 10,000. Now, let us say that the price drops down to $9,900. Again, you should buy bitcoins at the said lower price of $9,900. If the price decreases again, say, to USD 9850, you should make another buy order at the said lower price. Again, if the price drops down to, say, $9,700, you make another buy order, and so on and so forth. Okay, is this only buying a losing asset? If you just look at it like this, you can say that you are actually purchasing a cryptocurrency that keeps on losing its value. But, just imagine how much you would profit if the price of the cryptocurrency concerned (in this case, bitcoin) recovers and goes back to its original value ($10,000) or higher? When this happens, all your investments and buy orders will experience a nice profit. The good news is that such situation usually happens in the cryptocurrency market considering its highly volatile nature.

Before you use this strategy, it is important for you to identify a cryptocurrency whose value will most likely increase in the long run. For this purpose, you may want to use fundamental analysis. Keep in mind that your key to profit is when the price either goes back to its original price (the price when you first apply this strategy), or higher. Also, do not forget that although this strategy is very practical and effective, it is still an aggressive approach. In fact, this strategy is not recommended if you are a complete beginner. To minimize your risk, you may want to use a stop-loss limit. This is where you put a limitation as to how long you will keep on chasing a particular cryptocurrency. For example, you can set a stop-loss limit of 5, which means that you will only make up to 5 buy orders. After which, you will no longer make another buy order until its price recovers.

Coin Mastery

It is true that the more that you know and understand a particular cryptocurrency, the more likely that you can predict its price movement. This is exactly the focus of this strategy. When you use this approach, the key is to specialize in a single cryptocurrency of your choice. Make it a priority to find out as much as you can about that cryptocurrency. Be sure to research on it on a daily basis. Also, be updated with the latest news and developments regarding your chosen cryptocurrency. The important thing here is to achieve mastery over the cryptocurrency. This may take weeks and even months, but it is well worth it. After some time, you will notice that you are more able to predict its price movement. Once you achieve this level of understanding, then you can now make appropriate investments to make a profit. If you are convinced that you already have mastery over a particular cryptocurrency, them feel free to master another cryptocurrency. It should also be noted that while studying a particular cryptocurrency, you may realize that it is not a good investment at all. If you are sure about this, then feel free to abandon it and switch to another cryptocurrency that appears to be profitable.

Altcoin Spread Out

It is not a secret that you can make a big amount of profit by investing in altcoins. Some altcoins can increase by more than 500% in price within just a few weeks. In fact, many of such altcoins are almost unheard of. They operate without drawing so much attention but are highly lucrative investments. This strategy takes advantage of this kind of altcoins. The key is to spread your investments among different altcoins that have a high-profit potential. You do not have to profit from all.ofnthese investments. For example, if you make three different investments but make a 400% profit with one of them, even if you lose your other two investments, you will still end up at a profit. It is noteworthy that some altcoins even increase by more than 1,000%.

Of course, you are free to invest in major altcoins like Ethereum, but when you use this approach, it is suggested that you focus on minor altcoins. It is good to look at and study new altcoins in the market as they have a big room for improvements. Also, their price also tends to be so much cheaper, but their potential growth is high. Look for altcoins that offer value to the market. Find out if they are being promoted effectively and how the market responds to them. This way you will have an idea as to which altcoins to invest.

Go with the Flow

When China declared that it would close down all its local cryptocurrency exchanges, the price of bitcoin fell significantly. When Singapore issued that it will not yet impose any restriction on the use of cryptocurrencies, the price of bitcoin and other altcoins increased. When CNN featured a positive news piece that shows that bitcoin is a good investment, the price of bitcoin surged higher. When Russia decided to finally welcome the use of bitcoin, its price increased. As you can see, it is not difficult to predict how the price of a cryptocurrency will move. When there is positive news about a certain cryptocurrency, it tends to draw attention and interest. Usually, this will make the price of the cryptocurrency concerned to go higher. But, in case of bad news, then the contrary can be expected. When the co-founder of bitcoin sold his coins and invested in bitcoin cash, many people followed him. As a result, the price of bitcoin dropped, and the price of bitcoin cash increased significantly. The key to using this strategy is to get as much information as you can and see how such information will lead the market. Take note that it is not always advisable to just go with the flow all the time. You also need to analyze what is actually going on in the market.

Do not just rely on what the news says about a particular cryptocurrency. Also, you should be careful with people who use a pump and dump scheme. The pump and dump is usually applied in stocks, but it is also being applied to cryptocurrencies, especially to minor altcoins. So, how do a pump and dump work? Normally, a group of people will promote a certain cryptocurrency. They will even buy a big amount to show that its price is increasing. Now, this will convince other people to make an investment thinking that it is a nice investment. When this happens, its price will increase further. This is when the ones behind the scheme will sell whatever cryptocurrency they have promoted at a nice profit. What happens here is that all the other people who invested will end up holding a losing asset whose price has just dropped significantly. This is also the time when the victims will realize that they have not truly invested in something that is valuable. The pump and dump scheme is a fraudulent act. But, if you come to think of it, the price of the cryptocurrency that is made subject of the scheme does increase. Hence, if you can identify the proper timing as to when to buy and sell the said cryptocurrency, you can take advantage of the hard work of the people who are behind this fraudulent scheme and end up with a nice profit. Still, it is best to avoid anything that has to do with a pump and dump scheme.

Buy and Hold

The buy and hold strategy is a very simple strategy but is also highly effective. In fact, many of the people who became multimillionaires by investing in cryptocurrency used this strategy. So, how does it work? As the name implies, the buy and hold strategy means buying a particular cryptocurrency and then holding on to it as you wait for its price to increase. You can then sell it for profit after some time. Just how profitable can this strategy be? Again, let us use a classic example: Had you invested even just $400 in bitcoin way back in

2010, then you would have been a multimillionaire by now. Yes, this is how effective this strategy is.

When you use this strategy, it is important for you to choose a cryptocurrency whose price will most likely increase in the long run. Therefore, it is good to choose a strong cryptocurrency. A strong cryptocurrency is one that offers real value to the market. It should also have a wide and effective promotion, and it must have a high level of market acceptance. A good example of this would be bitcoin.

This strategy can be used for a short term, but it is more designed for a long-term investment. Since it is a long-term investment, you should expect to experience the usual fluctuations in the market. A common mistake is to panic and suddenly withdraw your investment, which could have been highly profitable had you been more patient. Some experts advise that you should learn to ignore your investment when you use this strategy. After all, if you are convinced that you have invested in a strong cryptocurrency, then you should trust in your investment. For example, bitcoin has also experienced many significant decreases in price, and yet it remains to be the number one and most successful cryptocurrency in the world. The power of this strategy lies in its simplicity. There are also real-life success stories of cryptocurrency millionaires who relied only on this simple strategy.

Quick Sell

This strategy relies on small yet continuous profits. When you use this strategy, it is important for you to exercise discipline and not be greedy. So, how does it work? The key is to close your position as soon as you experience a small profit. This way you can effectively minimize your risk and exposure. For example, you can buy 1 bitcoin. When the price of bitcoin increases in such a way that you gain a profit no matter how small, then sell it at a profit. This is also a good way to take advantage of the volatility of the market. Of course, when you use this strategy, you need to pick a strong cryptocurrency, so that there is a high probability that its price will most likely increase.

When you use this strategy, it is also advised that you use a stop-loss limit, so that you will know just up to what price you will continue to keep your investment. If you reach this limit, then accept losses and do not hesitate to close your position. This strategy is not hard to do, but you have to apply proper timing and be sure to close your position way before the price behavior changes. Again, you should not be greedy. Stick to earning continuous and small profits.

Chapter 5

Cryptocurrency Mining

A nother way of investing in cryptocurrency is by mining. Before a record (block) is added to the blockchain, the transaction must first be confirmed and verified. This is done by solving a difficult mathematical formula, and this process is referred to as mining. Miners are paid a fee for their work. Miners are important in order for transactions to be completed quickly. Hence, there is always a demand for miners. Mining cryptocurrency, especially Bitcoin, used to be very popular. Generally, there are three ways to mine cryptocurrency.

Although You can mine a cryptocurrency using your own computer alone, this is not a recommended approach as you will probably have to spend more on electricity than the amount of cryptocurrency that you can earn.This is because a computer does not have enough hash power for mining. Therefore, to increase your mining power, you need to use a mining hardware. This referred to as hardware mining. Take note that when you use a hardware, you will use it together with your computer. Now, there are two main issues when you use this approach. First, a powerful mining hardware can be very costly. It will take time for you to recover your cost for buying a mining hardware. The second issue is overheating. This is a serious issue as it can break both your mining hardware and your computer. To avoid this, you need to observe a schedule. Avoid mining for long hours as it can easily overheat and break your devices.

Another form of mining is known as software mining. This is where you install a certain software that you can use for mining. Your mining software provider payoff you to update your miners for a fee. This dispenses with the use of a hardware mining device. Still, you will have to use your computer every time you mine.

Last but not least, there is cloud mining. These days, many miners prefer this method as it offers the most convenience. With cloud mining, a mining company will do all the work for you. All you need to do is wait for the mining company to send you your cryptocurrencies. You do not even have to turn on your computer.

Okay, so what is the catch? Of course, this kind of deal is not for free. When you work with a mining company, you will have to pay the money company a certain amount. For example, pay 1 bitcoin and receive 0.05 BTC every week. Although this may seem like an excellent deal, unfortunately, it is not always the case. This is because what the mining company shows you is only the expected return and not the actual return. Hence, instead of getting 0.05 BTC, you might only receive 0.03 BTC, or even lower. Make sure that the terms and conditions of the contract are clear to you before you invest any real money. You should also pay attention to the duration of the contract. There are mining companies that make the contract effective for a lifetime while many limit it to a certain period like one year. Again, this depends on the terms and conditions of the contract. Another thing that you should be concerned about is the legitimacy of the mining company. The unfortunate truth is that there are many scammers out there. Even if you have a lifetime contract, there is nothing that you can profit if the mining company suddenly disappears or shuts down. Therefore, it is extremely important that you work with a reliable and legitimate mining company.

It is worth noting that many real experts suggest that if you are really serious about making money with cryptocurrencies, the better approach instead of mining is by investing in or trading cryptocurrencies.

Chapter 6

Best Investing
and Trading Practices

Use a Trading/Investing Journal

Although not considered a requirement, using a trading/investing journal can be very helpful. You do not have to be a writer just to keep a journal. However, there are two things that you need to observe: You need to be honest, and you need to update your trading journal regularly. Your journal should serve as a mirror of who you are as a cryptocurrency investor/trader. For this to happen, your journal should contain honest accounts and records of your experiences and lessons as a trader.

So, how can this be beneficial to you? As an investor or trader, it is important for you to learn to think outside the box. With the help of a trading journal, you will be able to view yourself from a new perspective, from a standpoint that is free from any form of bias or prejudice. This way you will be more able to identify your strengths and weaknesses. This is also a good way to discover ways to further develop your strategy.

If you are not fond of writing in a notebook, you can use a word file on your computer. If you want, you can even write everything on your mobile device. Just be sure not to lose the file where you write your journal. If you are a serious cryptocurrency investor or trader, it is strongly suggested that you use a journal.

Right Understanding of High Volatility

When people talk about cryptocurrencies, they always say that it has a high volatility. But, what does this really mean? High volatility means that a cryptocurrency's price can fluctuate and change significantly in a short period of time. Hence, the price of a cryptocurrency can drop by more than 50%quickly, even just in a few days. Conversely, its price can shoot up even by more than 100% in a week's time. Hence, there is a good side and a bad side when something has a high volatility. It will depend on the direction that the price of a cryptocurrency will take. However, the main problem with high volatility is people's understanding of it. Many still perceive it to be something that balances itself in the long run. Keep in mind that this is not how cryptocurrencies work. There is no automatic balancing factor. Therefore, it is wrong to think that a decrease in price will follow a significant increase in price. In the same way, a decrease in price does not always mean that the cryptocurrency's value will next increase. In fact, a decrease in price can still be followed by a series of decreases just as an increase in price can again be followed by multiple increases in value. This will all depend on how the cryptocurrency concerned performs in the market. Of course, there are many factors to consider, such as market acceptance, the economy, governments, market competition, and technological developments, among others. Still, do not view the high volatile nature of the cryptocurrency market as something bad. Do not forget that it is exactly this nature of the cryptocurrency market that makes it a highly profitable investment.

Another thing to take note of is that although you now understand what high volatility means, it does not mean that you can already predict its movement all the time. Sometimes no matter how much research you make, it is impossible to know how a certain cryptocurrency will move. This is normal. When this happens, just accept the fact that you cannot tell its movement *yet*. Just wait for the best timing when you are more certain of its price movement. Do not make half-hearted investments. You should be very confident with every investment to trade that you make. If you do not feel as confident, then it only means that the investment is not worth taking. Make sure that you use the high volatile nature of the cryptocurrency market in your favor and not the other way around. From time to time, you will have to be patient. Proper timing is essential to success.

Do Not Chase After Your Losses

There is a common advice that is given to casino gamblers, and that is not to chase after your losses. The reason is that chasing after your losses will most likely lead you to end up with more losses. What is surprising is that the people who fall into this trap are also the ones who are well aware that it is wrong to chase after one's losses. This is how tricky this pitfall is. So, for you to avoid this mistake, you need to understand what it actually means to chase after your losses. Normally, a person chases after his losses after experiencing a bad loss, such as when he loses a big trade. The tendency is to feel bad about it and has a strong will to recover what you have lost and still earn some profit. Since you will only earn a certain percentage of your investment, you will be tempted to suddenly invest a big amount, even all your remaining funds, in one investment or trade. The problem is that there is no amount of research or preparation that you can do to guarantee the outcome of any investment. You can only increase your chances of making a profit, but there is no 100‰ guarantee that an investment will end up with a positive return. After all, so many things can happen in the course of an investment. Now, the problem here is that you can still lose your subsequent trade or trades. It also changes your strategy into a highly aggressive one to the point that your overall funds may no longer be able to support your aggressive strategy. It should be noted that chasing after one's losses do not always lead to more losses. If you get lucky, you can even end up with a nice profit. However, the chances are that you will end up with a bad loss if you do apply this approach for a long term as it is too aggressive. Instead of chasing after your losses, you should focus on chasing after more profits. Admit and accept a loss when you encounter it, and remain calm. Learn from every mistake or losing trade that you experience and focus on developing your strategy. In the course of being a professional investor/trader, you will definitely make wrong decisions every now and then. That is normal. That is also how you will learn. Keep a positive mind and focus on making more profits. Make sure that every investment or trade that you make is backed up by sufficient research. Pay attention to the amount and quality of information that you have. When you deal with the cryptocurrency market, research should be a part of your day-to-day activity. This is because the cryptocurrency market is a continuously and quickly evolving market. You need to be up to date with the latest developments to for you to know the best strategy to use.

Sufficient Research

Every cryptocurrency investors or trader is well aware that doing research is important. However, a common mistake is not doing sufficient research. Just because you have read the news and stared at a graph for an hour do not mean that you can already come up with a sound trading decision. Highly successful and professional traders spend hours every day just to identify profitable cryptocurrencies to invest in.

Although there is no amount of research that can guarantee the outcome of an investment, it can significantly increase your chances of making the right investment decision. If you want to have continuous and long-term success as a cryptocurrency investor/trader, then doing sufficient research is an invaluable tool that you should always use.

But, just what amount of research is sufficient enough? There is no hard and fast rule as to the exact amount of research that you need to do. This will depend on various circumstances and the current situation of the market. You will know if you have done enough research if you have good reasons for making a trade or investment. The reasons that you have which should all be based on actual facts will also give you more confidence. You have to understand that the cryptocurrency market is not random. It is not a casino game. In fact, it is very scientific, and there are measurable factors that you can use to come up with a wise investment decision.

Follow the Latest News

As a cryptocurrency investor, you are expected to know what is going on in the market every day. Again this is part of fundamental analysis. Hence, you need to follow the latest news and developments. This is also a good way to discover other profitable cryptocurrency investments that you can make. You should not underestimate the power of the media, especially how certain cryptocurrencies get featured on major need channels. These news pieces have a solid impact on the price behavior of a cryptocurrency, so be sure to keep an eye on them. For example, when the news publicized that the co-founder of bitcoin sold all his coins and then invested in bitcoin cash, the price of bitcoin dropped, and the price of bitcoin cash increased really high. If you are aware of the said news, then the said outcome would have been very easy to predict. Of course, you should also be able to analyze the news and take advantage of it quickly.

Join Online Groups and Forums

It is also a good idea to join online groups and forums on cryptocurrencies. It is worth mentioning that cryptocurrency developers are also active in such places, so this is a good way to get valuable information even before it is released in public. This is also a good way to have an idea of how other cryptocurrency users think and respond to the market. Last but not least, joining online groups and forums can help you broaden your horizon and learn new and exciting ideas. You might even be able to meet interesting people who can help you achieve success. Online groups and forums are also excellent places to know the newest altcoins in the market. If you can identify a new yet promising altcoin, you can convert it into a highly lucrative investment.

If you get too friendly in this kind of environment, you may receive an invitation to join a particular group for a fee. It depends on you whether you want to join or not. Learn about the group as much as you can. Some of these groups are the ones who practice pump and dump with altcoins. Be careful because you might end up a victim of their scheme. Although some groups may help reveals to you vital and useful information, there are also those who simply want to make money from you. If you are a beginner, it is advised that you avoid joining any group that requires any form of payment, regardless of the amount, prior to being a member.

Professional Approach

There is nothing wrong with breaking into the cryptocurrency market as a hobby. In fact, this is how many people start out before they become a real professional. But, when you approach the market as a hobby, you should also not expect to earn a very high amount of profit from it. Having continuous and high amounts of profit in the cryptocurrency market usually demands dedication, time, patience, and commitment. Do not forget that every investment or trade that you make should be backed up by a rigorous study. At least, this is the way how professionals do it.

A common mistake to makes multiple trades even when you do not dedicate enough time to study the market. Instead of not taking it seriously, a better approach is to make fewer trades or investments. Just be sure that you research and study the market very well before you enter any position. Instead of considering it as a meet hobby, you should approach it professionally as you would any business or profession. This way you can avoid being too lazy and giving it less efforts than needed. How you approach the cryptocurrency market plays an important element in the outcome of a trade or investment. As a cryptocurrency investor/trader, you will usually get what you deserve depending on how much effort you put into every investment that you make. The more that you study and understand the market, the higher is your chance of making a profit.

Take a Break

The truth is that the activities of being a cryptocurrency investor/trader can be very addicting. It is not uncommon to find traders who do nothing but study the market and the different cryptocurrencies therein. And, mind you, this is a good thing. It shows dedication, passion, and commitment. All of these are essential to success. However, you should understand that taking a break is also an important factor. You will become more effective when you give yourself a chance to take a break and clear your mind. Hence, even though you are busy with your work as a cryptocurrency investor, make it also a priority to give yourself some time to relax every now and then. However, do not confuse taking a break with merely being lazy. Before you take any break or rest, make sure that you first do some serious work. Also, when you do take a break, do not be like the others who still think about their investments or ponder about a better strategy that they can use. That is still working and not resting. When you rest, do not even think about anything that is related to cryptocurrency. It is your time to just relax and enjoy life. Do not worry; after your break, you are expected to work more effectively and much harder.

Only Invest the Money that You Can Afford to Lose

This is a common advice that is normally given to casino gamblers. The same applies when you invest in cryptocurrencies, or even in any other kinds of investment. After all, every investment has its risks. Although your main objective is to make money, there is still the probability that you might lose all your capital, especially if you are not careful enough.

Remember to only invest the money that you can afford to lose. This means that you should not invest the money that you need to pay for your household bills, as well as other obligations. This way you will not be trading under pressure. As you may already know, trading under pressure is not good since you will not be able to think clearly and objectively. You should never allow your emotions to cloud your reasoning and judgment. When you use the money that you cannot afford to lose, the tendency is to feel pressured, and you will surely be affected if ever you lose a trade. To avoid these things from happening, you should only use the money that you can afford to lose. Do not worry; you do not need to have a big capital in your account right away. In fact, if you are just completely starting out, it is strongly recommended that you use the demo account provided by your broker (if you are trading) or just start out small.

Have a plan

There are cryptocurrency traders and investors who simply enter the market and hope to make a profit. The problem is that they do not have a plan. They only know what they want and nothing more. This is like going blind and entering a battlefield hoping that you will be the victor. True professional cryptocurrency investors always have a plan. Having a plan is also a good way to avoid trading under pressure or being too emotional. You should have a short-term plan and a long-term plan. Even before entering a position, you should already know just how much you intend to make from it. This is an effective way that will prevent you from being too greedy. The problem with greed is that it makes you lose not only the profit that you have already earned, but it can also take away your whole capital. Having a plan is the best way to combat greed. Needless to say, you need to stick to your plan. But, it should also be noted that the market keeps on changing, and so you should not be a slave to your plan. This is why you also have to make a long-term plan. You should prepare your position for any contingency that may arise. For example, even if your set plan is only to earn 50% of your investment, if it turns out that after attaining your 50% target the market still appears to be highly profitable, then you should reconsider your short-term plan and probably stick to your investment, which means switching to a long-term plan. Take note, however, that you should only abandon a plan if, and only *if*, there are good reasons to believe based on facts that the position that you have remains to be profitable.

But, what if the plan does not work? If the plan does not work, then admit any losses and just move on. Again, you should not chase after your losses. Instead, you have to learn from your mistakes, keep a positive mind, and continue to chase after more profits.

Request for a Withdrawal

There are many cryptocurrency investors and traders out there who do not make any withdrawal. The reason is that keeping their profits in their account will allow them to grow their funds and so earn a higher amount of profit. Obviously, a successful trade with a profit of 100% at the amount of 1 BTC and another successful trade at 2 BTC, although the profit percentage is the same at 100%, the one with a higher investment (2 BTC) will have a higher return. So, some investors and traders do not like to withdraw their profits so that they can have more funds which can earn a higher amount of profits. Now, although this may seem reasonable and practical, this is not a suggested approach. Keep in mind that the only way you can fully realize your profits is only when you can turn them into real cash. The only way to do this is by making a withdrawal; otherwise, it is as if you were just using a demo account. Also, by making a withdrawal, you get to minimize your exposure and risk. The thing is that as long as your cryptocurrency stays in your account or is not exchanged for cash, then there will always be a risk that it may lose its value. You do not need to withdraw all of your profits. You can still grow the funds that you use for trading or investing. If you want, you can just withdraw even just 25% of your profits every week or every month, depending on the kind of strategy that you are using.

Practice

Investing in or trading cryptocurrencies takes practice. You need to practice the strategies. It is not enough that you have just read of them. A good way to do this is by using a demo account or simply by starting out small. Continuous practice is important. The cryptocurrency market is a continuously evolving market, so you need to work on your strategy continuously. Also, the experience of actual trading or investing can be different from just reading about it in books. You should also develop your trading skills, and you do not learn skills just by reading. You need to expose yourself and engage in the actual practice. It also takes practice to be able to read graphs properly and predict the price movement of a cryptocurrency. The good news is that these things are learnable, but you need to spend time and effort to master them. The more that you practice and expose yourself to the cryptocurrency market the more that you will get good at investing/trading. Remember: practice makes perfect.

Conclusion

Thanks for making it through to the end of this book. We hope it was informative and able to provide you with all of the tools you need to achieve your goals whatever they may be.

The next step is to apply everything that you have learned and start earning profits with cryptocurrency. Many people have already earned a fortune by investing in it. To this day, the cryptocurrency market remains to be a highly lucrative place. By now, you should already be equipped with the right knowledge that can help you make a nice profit by investing in or trading cryptocurrencies.

Every day, some cryptocurrencies increase in value, which means that there is always a profit that you can make by investing in the cryptocurrency market. It is just a matter of identifying which cryptocurrency/cryptocurrencies to put your money in. There are already many people who have earned a fortune by investing or trading cryptocurrencies. Now is your turn to make positive changes in your life.

Finally, if you found this book useful in any way, a review on Amazon is always appreciated!

www.ingramcontent.com/pod-product-compliance
Lightning Source LLC
Chambersburg PA
CBHW072048230526
45468CB00019B/1044